£7.99

ISBN: 978-1-907823-30-5

Images © bigpictures.co.uk and Shutterstock.com

A Pillar Box Red Publication

we *love* you...

One Direction

A 2013 ANNUAL

Written by Sarah Milne
Designed by Nicky Regan

we ♥ you...

Contents

When Niall Horan, Zayn Malik, Louis Tomlinson, Harry Styles and Liam Payne stood in the queue for X Factor 2010 auditions, there's no way they could have imagined what was to become of them during the competition. From solo artists to group, from third place finalists to success in America, the boys have certainly done a lot in the short time they've known each other. Here's the story so far...

Obviously the boys impressed the judges at their first audition, and they made it through to the final stages of boot camp. But for one reason or another they were all rejected at this point, and denied the chance to go through to the judges' houses in the 'boys' category. But something about all five of them had made an impression on the judges, and in fact, it was guest judge Nicole Scherzinger that initially suggested forming them into a boy band for the 'groups' category – a category which for that year had been particularly weak.

Thrown together, the boys were shocked but delighted to have been given a second chance. For Liam especially this was good news – he'd once before auditioned for the show in 2008 at aged just 14, getting through to the judges houses. But he was sent home before the live shows because Simon Cowell thought he was just not ready – a huge disappointment at the time, but without that initial rejection, One Direction as we know them today would not have existed.

After the initial excitement, there was much work to be done – the boys had just 5 weeks to turn themselves from solo artists into a band! They all lived at different ends of the country, so things were a bit tricky – at one point the boys moved into a house at the bottom of Harry's stepfather's garden. They sang their hearts out, but it was a tough time for all – they weren't sure which direction (ha) they should be going in and most importantly of all, they couldn't agree on a name.

Then Harry came up with One Direction, mainly because he thought it would sound cool when the X Factor announcer said it in his deep voice. The rest of the boys loved it, and it stuck. They were finally on the way to becoming a band.

At Simon Cowell's house, the first song they performed for him as a group was Natalie Imbruglia's 'Torn'. Simon admitted that he was keeping a straight face for the sake of the camera, but that he immediately knew that the boys would be a hit – they'd worked hard, come together as a group, and as friends, and blown his socks off!

One Direction Beginnings

The live shows had their ups and downs for One Direction, but in general, they were given good feedback, and their faithful band of fans, Directioners, was growing every week. When they made it through to the final three, everyone was disappointed to see them come third after Rebecca Ferguson and Matt Cardle, the eventual winner.

Almost as soon as the winner was announced, the song One Direction would have released had they won was leaked onto the internet.

The boys were obviously gutted to have lost, but the hard work they'd put in over the previous months was not going to waste- they were certain they would carry on as a group and try to find success on their own.

And find success they did – in January 2011, they signed a £2 million record contract with Simon Cowell's label

Syco. The rest of 2011 just got better, with singles and their first album released, as well as their first sellout tour – Up All Night.

2012 has seen the boys crack the tricky American market, becoming the first UK boy band to do so since The Beatles! They have also recorded their second album, due for release in 2013, as well as announced a World Tour in 2013 too. The second album is rumoured to be grungier than the first, with more guitars – rock!

One Direction certainly are very busy boys at the moment, but we love them because their friendship, sense of humour and cheeky good looks all come together to make their singing talent even better. Long may they continue – we look forward to seeing how they develop as artists and friends!

One Direction
Beginnings

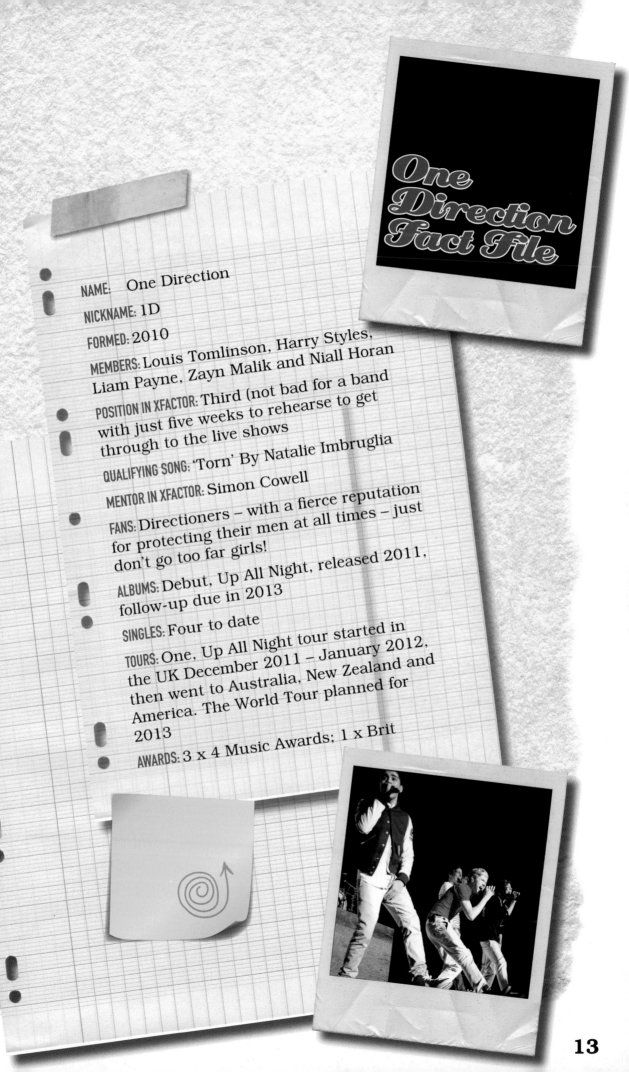

One Direction Fact File

NAME: One Direction

NICKNAME: 1D

FORMED: 2010

MEMBERS: Louis Tomlinson, Harry Styles, Liam Payne, Zayn Malik and Niall Horan

POSITION IN XFACTOR: Third (not bad for a band with just five weeks to rehearse to get through to the live shows

QUALIFYING SONG: 'Torn' By Natalie Imbruglia

MENTOR IN XFACTOR: Simon Cowell

FANS: Directioners – with a fierce reputation for protecting their men at all times – just don't go too far girls!

ALBUMS: Debut, Up All Night, released 2011, follow-up due in 2013

SINGLES: Four to date

TOURS: One, Up All Night tour started in the UK December 2011 – January 2012, then went to Australia, New Zealand and America. The World Tour planned for 2013

AWARDS: 3 x 4 Music Awards; 1 x Brit

NAME: Niall James Horan

BORN: 13 September 1993

STARSIGN: Virgo

HOMETOWN: Mullingar, Ireland.

FAMILY: Mum Maura, Dad Bobby, older brother Greg.

MUSICAL TALENTS: Niall was in the school choir, where he loved performing, and he has also been playing guitar since he was around 11 years old. He likes to write music and lyrics. He described his first guitar, a gift one Christmas, as the best present ever.

LIKES: Lots of different types of music – swing, rock, old, new – if it's well written with a great tune, Niall's a fan.

DISLIKES: Clowns and being hungry.

FUN FACT: Niall's family only realised what a great singer he was when they were in the car and thought that the radio was playing – in fact it was Niall singing!

Niall Horan Biog

we love you...

```
R Q L F Y S T T J Y Z N V
N L M R H R R E T T I W T
Y T R W V E L L O U I S L
L A B M X N I N Q D V T O
H Y E N B O A N R T D C K
L R A Q Q I M S V G Y C M
Q O U H P T Z P E S N K V
W T T L R C R A J O T R F
P C I M V E P W Y T R N M
M A F T J R R L D N I E C
M F U R K I T F Z A F T H
N X L Z P D L R L M K Z T
K D Y C N C O L U M B I A
```

Wordsearch

Find the words in the grid. Words can go horizontally, vertically and diagonally in all eight directions.

Answers can be found on page 60 - 61.

Beautiful

Columbia

Directioners

Heroes

Harry

Liam

Louis ♡

Niall

Syco

Twitter

Xfactor

Zayn

NAME: Zayn Javadd Malik

BORN: 12 January 1993

STARSIGN: Capricorn

HOMETOWN: Bradford, England

FAMILY: Mum Tricia, Dad Yaser, sisters Doniya, Waliyha and Safaa

MUSICAL TALENTS: R&B and rap

MUSICAL INFLUENCES: Bruno Mars

LIKES: His hair – his daily routine includes blowdrying and a bit of hairspray – Zayn's been proud of his appearance since he was a young boy.

DISLIKES: Open water – Zayn can't swim! He also doesn't like sandwich crusts, preferring his to be cut off.

FUN FACT: His favourite Avenger is The Hulk – you won't like him when he's angry. Zayn's choice of song to serenade his favourite girl would be 'Let Me Love You' by Mario, the song he performed for his first X Factor audition.

we love you... Zayn

Zayn Malik Biog

Answers can be found on page 60 - 61.

Crossword

ACROSS

4 The boys have marched into the US, being dubbed the British .... (8)

7 This Natalie Imbruglia song took the boys form the judges houses to the live shows (4)

10 No sleep listening to the 1D album (2, 3, 5)

11 The boys X Factor mentor, and now record label boss, Simon .... (6)

13 British singer/songwriter, behind the 1D song 'Moments', Ed .... (7)

14 The oldest member of the group once worked as a waiter for Doncaster Rovers (5)

DOWN

1 The boys sold out 6 nights at this venue on their first tour, O2 .... (5)

2 Debut single, 'What Makes You ....' (9)

3 '........... Be You', boys second single (5)

5 1D superfans (12)

6 Zayn's most recent tattoo has a very musical theme (10)

8 This band member has Irish eyes (5)

9 Liam has only one of these working in his body! (6)

12 Harry was a member of this chilly group before auditioning for X Factor, White .... (6)

NAME: Liam James Payne

BORN: 29 August 1993

STARSIGN: Virgo

HOMETOWN: Wolverhampton, England

FAMILY: Mum Karen, Dad Geoff, older sisters Ruth and Nicola.

MUSICAL TALENTS: Studied Music Technology at City of Wolverhampton College.

MUSICAL INFLUENCES: Justin Timberlake, Gary Barlow.

LIKES: Keeping fit. Since he was a baby, Liam has had health issues with his kidneys, and as a child had to have 32 injections every morning and evening to help him cope. Now, only one of his kidneys is working, so he has to take extra care of his health.

DISLIKES: Bullying – he suffered in high school, and took up boxing as a way to learn how to defend himself and to give him self-confidence.

FUN FACT: He likes happy, smiley girls, owns a pair of pink hair straighteners and likes to put on lots of aftershave after singing in the shower.

Liam Payne Biog

One Direction Live!

NAME:	Harry Edward Styles
BORN:	1 February 1994
STARSIGN:	Aquarius
HOMETOWN:	Holmes Chapel, Cheshire
FAMILY:	Mum Anne, Dad Des, older sister Gemma

MUSICAL TALENTS: Lead singer with the band White Eskimo – the band won a battle of the bands competition before Harry auditioned for the X Factor.

MUSICAL INFLUENCES: Elvis Presley, The Beatles, Kings of Leon, Coldplay.

LIKES: The ladies – as well as a well-publicised spell with (much) older ex-girlfriend Caroline Flack, Harry has expressed an interest in hotties Kim Kardashian and Katherine Schwarzenegger.

DISLIKES: Bullying – Harry's recently been subjected to some nasty comments on his Twitter account, sadly some of them coming from people in his hometown – no doubt jealous of their former classmate's huge success. He's learned to ignore these, but still it must hurt.

FUN FACT: Harry has a star tattoo on the side of his arm, which shows five stars representing the five members of One Direction. Harry is scared of snakes.

Harry Styles Biog

1. Which member of One Direction named the band, after thinking that it would sound good when read by the X Factor announcer?

Harry

2. Which member of the band had previously auditioned for X Factor?

Liam

3. And, at what stage was he eliminated?

Juges horusos rightbeforliveshow

4. Which British singer/songwriter wrote the song 'Moments'?

ED Sheeran

5. Who described the boys as being like the new Take That?

simon cowell

20 Questions

6. What are the boys' middle names?

Janus Javadd James william

7. Who or what is White Eskimo?

8. What accolade did One Direction's first book, *One Direction: Forever Young (Our Official X Factor Story)* get?

9. What has One Direction's huge success in America been nicknamed?

10. How much was their record contract with Syco records worth?

11. Which show did One Direction make their American Debut?

12. And where was it recorded – having to move there to cope with audience demands?

13. Which instrument is the band's second album rumoured to contain more of?

14. Which member of the band has a phobia of spoons?

15. And which One Direction member is scared of snakes?

16. Who would the boys love to work with next?

17. Which band did One Direction support on their first US tour?

18. Which of the band is left-handed?

19. Who changed their name, replacing an 'i' with a 'y', thinking it more original?

20. Which member of the band has a cameo in the video for Ed Sheeran's hit 'Drunk'?

we love you...
Louis

NAME: Louis William Tomlinson, born Louis Troy Austin (he took his stepfather's name when his mum remarried).

BORN: 24 December 1991

STARSIGN: Capricorn

HOMETOWN: Doncaster, Yorkshire

FAMILY: Mum Johannah, Dad Troy, Stepdad Mark, five half-sisters, Georgia, Charlotte, Félicité, and twins Daisy and Phoebe.

MUSICAL PAST: Played the lead role of delicious Danny Zuko in a school production of Grease the Musical.

MUSICAL INFLUENCES: Robbie Williams, Ed Sheeran, The Fray.

LIKES: Bandmate Harry – he has a picture of the two of them together on his bedside table. 'Proper' relationships – Louis isn't into the idea of short flings or one-night stands.

DISLIKES: Girls that are too goody two shoes. Haters – he just tries to turn any negative situation into the positive by using his cheeky sense of humour.

FUN FACTS: Louis loves wearing stripes so much he tries to ban the other band members from wearing them. Louis once got dumped because he wasn't attractive enough!

Louis Tomlinson Biog

OK, so One Direction only released their debut single in 2011, but since then, the boys have been busy writing performing and touring. In 2012, the album Up All Night debuted in the US Billboard charts at Number 1 – the first ever UK act in the history of the Billboard charts to do so.

Their 2nd album was recorded in Sweden in May 2012, and promises to be a slight change in direction – more guitars and grungier.

What they've done so far is impressive, so we can't *wait* to see what they do next!

WHAMM!

ALBUMS

Up All Night – released 18 November 2011 – to date has sold over 2 million copies and become 3 x Platinum seller in Australia and Ireland, 2 x Platinum in New Zealand and Gold in Sweden and UK.

BOOOMM!!

1D Discography

SINGLES: 2011

What Makes You Beautiful – Reached number 1 in UK charts. 5 x Platinum in Australia, 2 x Platinum in Canada, New Zealand and US.

Gotta Be You: Tricky second single, reached number 3 in UK and Irish charts.

KRASH!

SINGLES AS GUEST ARTIST

Both of these were charity singles.

2010

Heroes (release by XFactor finalists): Reached number 1 in UK and Irish Charts.

2011

Wishing on A Star (released by JLS and XFactor finalists): Reached number 1 in UK and Irish Charts.

MUSIC VIDEOS

One Direction have made three music videos to date, for singles **What Makes You Beautiful**, **Gotta Be You** and **Up All Night**.

SINGLES: 2012

One Thing – Reached number 9 in UK charts. 2 x Platinum in Australia and Gold in New Zealand.

More Than This – Reached only number 86 in UK charts.

we love you...

we love you...

Even the most successful British band, with hits in UK, Europe and Australia can find it impossible to crack America – even the daddy of all boy bands, Take That, have never really conquered the States.

The British Invasion:

ONE DIRECTION TAKE OVER THE US

In fact, The Beatles were the last British boy band to capture the hearts and minds of the American youth. Until One Direction came along that is!

We all know that the boys are talented and hard-working, but it seems like a little bit of good timing has been partly responsible for their American successes. After signing in the UK to Syco, Simon Cowell's record label, at the start of 2011, the boys were then signed by the massive Columbia records in the US. Record company bosses and music critics alike recognised that while Justin Bieber was still a massive solo artist for that type

of music and fans, there was no boy band like him. One Direction were cute, wholesome, cheeky and great singers – a perfect fit!

The boys first appeared on US TV in January 2012, on the massive The Today Show. As they hadn't released any records over there yet, the producers of the show thought it would just be another small performance by an unknown band. Once the fans found out though – the show's production team was inundated with emails about the appearance and they decided to move the boys from appearing in the studio to the larger venue Rockefeller Center, allowing fans to watch

the performance. They said that only Lady Gaga, Justin Bieber and Chris Brown have created a bigger stir than One Direction – and they were already established artists, the boys hadn't even released a single at that point!

When *Up All Night* was eventually released in the US, it went straight in at number 1 on the Billboard charts – the first British band ever to do this!

A tour of the US in summer 2012 further cemented the boys as a band to follow, and 1D saw themselves pelted with bras by some enthusiastic fans!

The boys may have broken America, but there will be a lot of hard work to keep the US fans happy – but it's going to be worth it. One record company insider estimated that success in America would be worth $100 million to the boys! Sounds like a good pay packet to us – we'll just have to watch this space and see if it becomes the United States of One Direction!

Zayn wears his celeb crush on his chest with this great Katy Perry sweatshirt. He's managing to pull off the two earrings look too.

Low key and casual, but still bang on trend – Niall's rocking the big trainers and hoody look - smartening it up with a dark grey blazer.

ZAYN

we love you...

One Direction Style...

we love you...

NIALL

Harry's looking like a typical English gent in this bow tie and grey tweed blazer. He's sure to attract some classy attention in this getup.

we love you...

HARRY

Liam is casual but cool with this checked lumberjack shirt, chinos and dazzling white trainers.

LIAM

Where's Wally? Oh, you mean that's actually Louis? We're not sure he really needs those glasses, but they certainly create a 'look'. Love the rest of the outfit though – stripes really suit him.

Ah, Louis – always the one for the big fashion statements. Yes, we love a onesie too, but would we wear it out and about? Luckily Louis has the natural flair to pull it off.

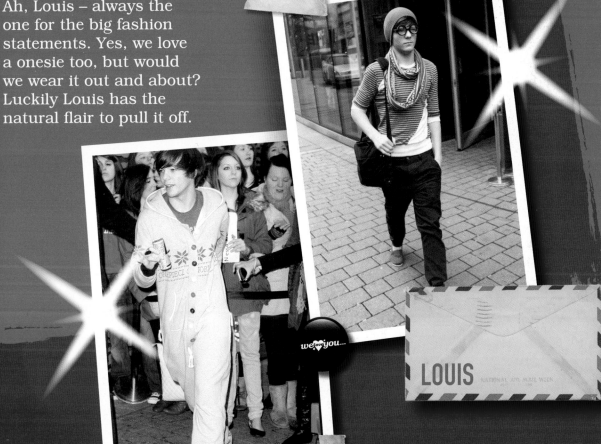

LOUIS

we ♥ you...

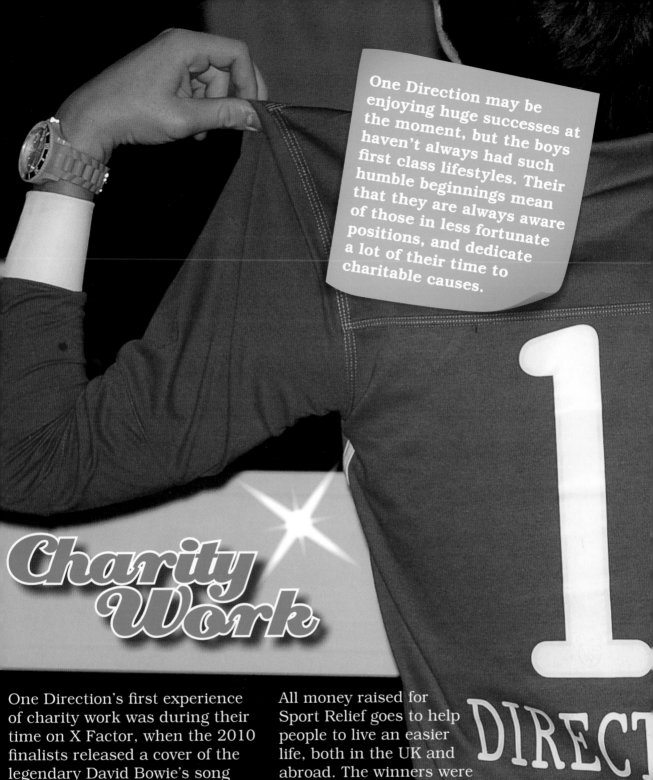

One Direction may be enjoying huge successes at the moment, but the boys haven't always had such first class lifestyles. Their humble beginnings mean that they are always aware of those in less fortunate positions, and dedicate a lot of their time to charitable causes.

Charity Work

One Direction's first experience of charity work was during their time on X Factor, when the 2010 finalists released a cover of the legendary David Bowie's song 'Heroes' in aid of Help for Heroes, the charity which aims to help provide better facilities for British servicemen and women wounded in the line of duty. All 16 original finalists recorded the single and it was released in November 2012 and went straight to the top of the charts in both UK and Ireland.

In early 2012, the boys took part in Sport Relief, offering themselves for auction via Twitter for the 'Twitrelief' campaign.

All money raised for Sport Relief goes to help people to live an easier life, both in the UK and abroad. The winners were followed and retweeted by all the boys on Twitter.

1D have also been showing off their culinary skills, providing a recipe for new cookbook, Dish for a Wish, produced by Rays of Sunshine, a charity which grants wishes to very ill children in the UK.

The boys sold VIP tickets to their US tour, and gave the proceeds to Great Ormond Street Hospital children's charity.

One Direction Merchandise & Endorsements

The hard work of a modern boy band doesn't just stop at the selling of singles, albums and tour tickets.

Oh no – today's pop stars have to work hard for their money, and One Direction are no exception. Known to be extremely hard workers – no doubt due to the beady eye of their X Factor mentor Simon Cowell – the boys have branched out to other lines, and so here's a list of the latest One Direction approved products...

ONE DIRECTION DOLLS: of course, all 30cm tall and with faces created using the latest laser technology for added accuracy.

POKÉMON: One Direction became brand ambassadors for Pokémon Black and White in April 2011, and was featured playing the game in TV ads.

NOKIA: The boys launched two limited edition phones for the mobile phone giant. The phones contained exclusive content such as One Direction wallpapers, ringtones, and behind the scenes videos of the band.

CALENDAR: the One Direction 2012 Calendar became the top selling calendar of all time, according to amazon.com

BOOK: One Direction: Forever Young (Our Official X Factor Story) was released on 17 February 2011

and reached the number one spot on the Sunday Times Bestseller list.

STILL TO COME: toys, games and entertainment products, including dolls and mini-figures of the One Direction members are in development – get them on your Christmas list now!

Meet the Fans!

1. Baby you light up my world like nobody else,
The way that you flip your hair gets me overwhelmed,
But when you smile at the ground it ain't hard to tell.

That's what makes you beautiful

2. Don't even care about the table breaking
We only wanna have a laugh
I'm only thinking 'bout this girl I'm seeing
I hope she'll wanna kiss me back.

up all night

3. Wake up, we both need to wake up
Maybe if we face up to this
We can make it through this.

Same mistakes

4. It's hard to get old without a cause,
I don't want to perish like a fading horse,
Youth is like diamonds in the sun,
And diamonds are forever.

Forever young

5. Tell me I'm a screwed up mess
That I never listen, listen
Tell me you don't want my kiss
That you need your distance, distance.

tell me a lie

6. And as you close your eyes tonight,
I pray that you will see the light,
That's shining from the stars above...

More than this

7. You've got everything you need

But you want accessories

Got to hold it in your hand

If I changed the world for you

I bet you wouldn't have a clue

I want

8. Under the lights tonight

You turned around, and you stole my heart

With just one look, when I saw your face

I fell in love

stle my heart

9. Now girl I hear it in your voice and how it trembles

When you speak to me I don't resemble who I was

You've almost had enough

gotta be you

10. I know your heart's been broken

But don't you give up

I'll be there, yeah I know it

To fix you with love

stand up

Answers can be found on page 60 - 61.

Name That Tune

ONE DIRECTION LYRICS

* Harry's favourite TV show is Family Guy and his favourite movie is Love Actually.

* If Louis had a superpower, he would fly.

* Louis' favourite band is The Fray.

* Louis' celebrity crush is Diana Vickers and his man crush is Robbie Williams.

* Liam's favourite colour is purple.

* Liam's favourite film is the Toy Story trilogy.

* Liam's celebrity crush is Leona Lewis and his man crush is stand-up comedian Michael McIntyre.

* Liam has a very unusual phobia, of spoons.

* Niall's ideal woman is Cheryl Cole and his man crush is Michael Buble.

* Niall's favourite movie of all time is Grease.

* Niall is left-handed.

* On their 53:14min long debut album 'Up All Night', Harry gets 7:18min worth of solos, Liam has 7:08min, Zayn has 5:38min, Louis has 1:29min and Niall has 1:24min.

* Zayn fancies Megan Fox and has a secret man crush on Justin Timberlake.

* Zayn's favourite book is Harry Potter.

* Zayn can't swim.

* The band's Twitter ID's are @Harry_Styles, @NiallOfficial, @zaynmalik, @Real_Liam_Payne and @Louis_Tomlinson.

* It was guest judge, former Pussycat Doll Nicole Scherzinger, who suggested that Harry, Niall, Zayn, Liam and Louis should be put together as a group at X Factor bootcamp.

* Harry came up with the band name One Direction.

* One Direction's 2011/2012 UK tour sold out in just 12 minutes when tickets went on sale.

* Liam loves boxing.

* Niall says he's only read one book – the American classic 'To Kill a Mockingbird'.

* Niall has a very bizarre go1D lucky mascot – a pair of white socks.

* Liam once confessed to owning a pair of pink hair straighteners.

* Niall is an accomplished guitar player while Harry plays the kazoo!

* To date 'What Makes You Beautiful', 'Gotta Be You' and 'One Thing' have amassed over 70million views altogether on YouTube. Impressive!

* The One Direction dolls are all 30cm in height and were created using laser-image face-sculpts for maximum authenticity.

* Harry makes a brief cameo appearance in Ed Sheeran's first 'Drunk' video. It was filmed backstage at London's Shepherd's Bush Empire.

* One Direction have a bizarre pre-gig ritual of eating Haribo sweets together. Louis explained to The Sun: "We do the sweets like they're drinks. We 'cheers them'. It's very strange but it's for good luck."

* Zayn's favourite song is 'Thriller' by Michael Jackson, Harry loves 'Shine On You Crazy Diamond' by Pink Floyd, Louis' choice is 'Look After You' by The Fray while Niall's is Coldplay's 'Viva La Vida'. Liam prefers 'Happy Birthday' as it means he will open presents.

Trivia

"Sometimes you feel the song's the star, but it's not like that here – it's the act, It's a real moment."

SONNY TAKHAR, MD SYCO RECORDS

INTERVIEWER: *Miley Cyrus or Selena Gomez?*

LOUIS TOMLINSON: *I'd rather say Eleanor Calder.*

"I can't work properly without my uh, without my boys. It just doesn't feel right."

HARRY STYLES

"When they came to my house in Spain and performed, after about a millionth of a second I knew they were sensational. I tried to keep a straight face for a bit of drama for the show. I remember sitting next to this girl who I was working with. The second they left we jumped out of my chair and said, "These guys are incredible!" They just had it. They had this confidence. They were fun. They worked out the arrangements themselves. They were like a gang of friends, and kind of fearless as well."

SIMON COWELL

"Social media has become the new radio, it's never broken an act globally like this before. These guys live online, and so do their fans."

WILL BLOOMFIELD, ONE DIRECTION'S MANAGER

INTERVIEWER: *Are you a fan of Harry Potter?*

HARRY STYLES: *Yeah, massive fan.*

LIAM PAYNE: *That's why his name is Harry.*

"We're the nudest people ever. Harry's nudity is contagious."

NIALL HORAN

"I want a girlfriend I can call in the middle of the night, I'd love that!"

HARRY STYLES

"If only our fans know how badly I want to meet them and hug them."

NIALL HORAN

(There's still a market for) "clean cut, wholesome, middle class parent friendly pop: cute boys advocating puppy love. And what could be better than one cute boy, if not five?"

NEIL MCCORMICK,
THE DAILY TELEGRAPH

"I feel like Niall is my little brother, because I always think he is the youngest in the band."

LIAM PAYNE

"There's a lot of possibility here, there's a lot of upside, that level of talent with those kinds of looks, it's really a perfect storm for a massive, massive successful phenomenon."

BILL WERDE,
FROM BILLBOARD MAGAZINE

"The day in which Niall shares his food with a girl, we'll know she's right for him."

LOUIS TOMLINSON

"Harry watched Titanic 10 times, and at the end, he always cries."

NIALL HORAN

"We are ourselves. People enjoy what we do because we don't hide anything."

LIAM PAYNE

"One Direction fans, thanks for supporting us from the very start... and appreciating five complete idiots!"

ZAYN MALIK

Quotes

Influences

While some may see One Direction as a manufactured boy band, all five members have a great interest in all types of music – and clearly they love to sing too. Here are a few of the artists that have inspired each of the members separately and as a group.

NIALL

Michael Buble: Niall's family discovered he could sing the same way Michael Buble's did – when they were both singing in the car.

Frank Sinatra and Dean Martin: Classic Rat Pack swing singers, these two are hard to beat.

Ed Sheeran: Niall was delighted to collaborate with Ed on their song Moments.

The Eagles, Bon Jovi, The Script: Niall has a rockier edge and loves these bands.

Beyonce and Justin Bieber: during his XFactor audition, Niall said he wanted to be as big as these stars.

ZAYN

Mario: Zayn loves R&B and rap, and performed Mario's Let Me Love You for his XFactor audition.

Bruno Mars: Zayn's dream collaborator.

LIAM

Justin Timberlake: Liam really rates the all round skills of JT.

Gary Barlow: Liam loves to watch and take inspiration from Gary Barlow's live performances.

HARRY

Elvis Presley: The King – another artist to send female fans screaming for more.

The Beatles: A great British band and a strong influence for Harry.

Foster the People, Coldplay, Kings of Leon: Harry likes more indie bands, and One Direction even covered Kings of Leon hit "Use Somebody" on their tour.

LOUIS

Robbie Williams: Louis loves Robbie's energy and enthusiasm for performance.

Ed Sheeran: A great inspiration on the songwriting side of things.

A to Z

A AUSTRALIA
The lads are huge down under, selling more records there to date than anywhere else.

B BRITISH INVASION
How One Direction's success in America has been described.

C COLUMBIA
Massive US record label, who One Direction signed with.

D DIRECTIONERS
Their most loyal fans.

E ED SHEERAN
Collaborating with this singer/songwriter was a dream come true for the boys.

F FUN
All the One Direction boys love what they do, and above all, like to have fun while they work. Their cheeky personalities shine through at all their interviews.

G GIRLS
The boys certainly like the female attention. At their summer tour of the US, they were pelted with bras while performing on stage.

H HARRY
His hair, his eyes, that cheeky grin – we can't help but love Mr Styles.

I IRELAND
1D are huge in Niall's homeland, where everyone was behind the boys to win X Factor.

J JUSTINS
Bieber and Timberlake – both these superstars are inspirational to the boys.

K KINGS OF LEON
Harry especially is a huge fan of KoL, and the band have covered "Somebody Like Me', in their live set.

L LIAM
Second time lucky for our Liam – he first auditioned for XFactor in 2008, aged just 14.

L (AGAIN) LOUIS
The eldest of the group once had a job as a waiter at Doncaster Football Club.

M MORE THAN THIS
Ballad confirmed to be the next single from their album.

N NIALL
Loves performing, and has plenty of talent, as well as that famous Irish charm.

O O2 ARENA
For the boys' 2013 World Tour they've already sold out 6 nights at the O2 Arena.

P POKÉMON
One Direction became brand ambassadors for this game in 2011.

Q QUESTIONS
The boys are usually very honest when anyone asks them a question, but still like to poke fun at interviewers every now and again.

R ROCK
Both Niall and Harry love a bit of rock, from The Eagles to Bon Jovi.

S SIMON COWELL
Their X Factor mentor, the boys signed to Syco, his record company in January 2011 for a £2 million record contract.

T THIRD PLACE
They may have won the bronze medal in the XFactor final, but the boys have done much better than their rivals!

U UP ALL NIGHT
First Album, went straight to number 1 in the US Billboard charts – the first ever British band to do this.

V VALERIE
The band covered The Zutons' song live.

W WHAT MAKES YOU BEAUTIFUL
Debut single, sold over half a million records in the UK in 2011.

X X FACTOR
The show that started it all.

Y YUMMY
Each one of the boys has their own individual personality and characteristics, but we love them all.

Z LAST BUT NOT LEAST, ZAYN
Of course!

Spot the Difference

CAN YOU SPOT 10 DIFFERENCES BETWEEN THESE 2 ONE DIRECTION PICS?

The boys may be young and the band just on its second album, but that doesn't stop One Direction wanting to work with some of the best musical talent around. Here are some of the people they've already worked with as well as some they'd like to collaborate with in future.

ED SHEERAN: Singer/songwriter Ed Sheeran wrote the boys' song 'Moments', and offered it to the band after meeting Harry at his guitarist's friends house. He had written it years before but never thought he was going to use it. Ed is now looking forward to working with 1D again in the future and says that he has sent them two new songs as a start.

SAVAN KOTECHA: the award-winning American songwriter and producer worked on 'What Makes You Beautiful" and 'One Thing'. He's also written for Usher, Britney Spears and Justin Bieber, as well as being lead vocal coach on X Factor 2010.

TOM FLETCHER: Ex McFly singer and guitarist, Tom wrote the song 'I Want' for One Direction's new album.

KELLY CLARKSON: First American Idol winner Kelly co-wrote "Tell Me a Lie" from 'Up All Night'.

NATALIE
IMBRUGLIA
→

GYM CLASS
HEROES
←

Collaborations & Covers

KINGS
OF LEON
→

BLACK
EYED PEAS
←

Covers

While on the X Factor, the boys performed songs by Pink, Coldplay, The Beatles, Elton John, Kelly Clarkson, Snow Patrol and Rihanna.

Live, the boys have been known to feature a whole range of songs by other artists, and usually ones they are fans of. Notable covers include:

KINGS OF LEON: Use Somebody

NATALIE IMBRUGLIA: Torn

GYM CLASS HEROES: Stereo Hearts

THE ZUTONS: Valerie

THE BLACK EYED PEAS: I Gotta Feeling

P17: WORDSEARCH

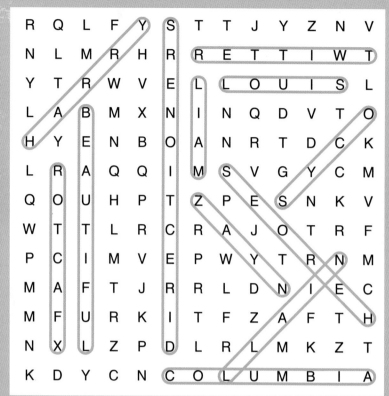

P28: 20 QUESTIONS

1. *Harry*
2. *Liam*
3. *Judges houses, right before the live shows*
4. *Ed Sheeran*
5. *Simon Cowell*
6. *James (Niall), Javadd (Zayn), James (Liam), Edward (Harry), William (Louis)*
7. *The band Harry was lead singer for before auditioning at XFactor*
8. *Number 1 on the Sunday Times Bestseller list - ooer!*
9. *The British Invasion*
10. *A cool £2 million!*
11. *The Today Show*
12. *The Rockefeller Center – the boys' appearance drew the same crowds as Justin Bieber, Lady Gaga and Chris Brown*
13. *More guitars, giving the boys a grungier sound - we can't wait!*
14. *Liam*
15. *Harry*
16. *Bruno Mars*
17. *Big Time Rush*
18. *Niall*
19. *Zayn (originally called Zain)*
20. *Harry*

P21: CROSSWORD

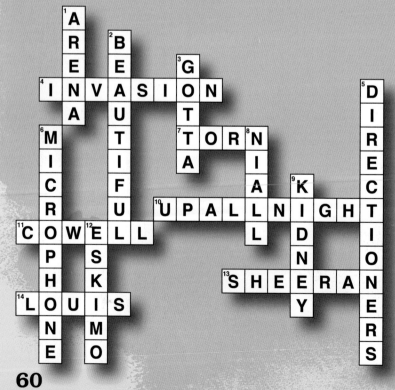

P46: NAME THAT TUNE

Quiz Answers

P57: SPOT THE DIFFERENCE

Where's Harry?